Copyright © 2024 by Elsa Mercier
All rights reserved.
No portion of this book may be reproduced in any form without written permission from the author.

Table of Contents

0. INTRODUCTION   3

1. THE FOUNDATIONS OF YOUR GLOW UP

Visualize the woman you want to become	6
Harness the power of the Law of Attraction	10
Take responsibility for your life	20

2. MANAGING YOUR EMOTIONS

Never let others influence your inner peace	26
Stop trying to control everything	27
You are not responsible for others' emotions	32
Never take things personally	33
Learn to manage your stress and anxiety	36

3. BOOSTING YOUR SELF-CONFIDENCE AND SELF-LOVE

It's time to recognize your worth	46
Reprogram your subconscious mind	49
Live for yourself, not for others	59
Be the "main character" of your life	62
Take care of yourself and your mental health	66

4. CREATING A HEALTHY AND POSITIVE ENVIRONMENT

Protect your personal space at all costs	76
Build a quality social circle	83
Learn to stop giving a sh*t	88
Be mindful of the impact of social media	91

5. DEVELOPING YOUR DISCIPLINE AND RESILIENCE

Create a morning routine that will boost your day	94
Set goals and stick to them	96
Stop procrastinating	102
Nothing extraordinary happens in your comfort zone	105
To succeed, you must fail	109

INTRODUCTION

Before we dive in...

If you're holding this book in your hands, it means you're not yet the woman you want to be. But you know what? That woman- the one who seems out of reach right now- she already exists within you. She's just waiting to be revealed. And that's precisely the purpose of this book: to help you unlock your full potential and become the woman you dream of being.

If you don't know me yet, my name is Elsa Mercier. For years, I felt stuck in a version of myself that didn't match my dreams or the person I knew I could be. I was extremely anxious, lacked self-confidence, and had a hard time asserting myself. I didn't resemble the confident, determined, resilient, and fulfilled woman I am today.

In the following pages, I will share all the advice, tools, and lessons you need to take your life to the next level. You will learn to cultivate unshakeable self-confidence, take control of your thoughts and emotions, transform failures into opportunities, and move toward your goals with unwavering determination.

You will become a woman who radiates self-confidence, knows exactly what she wants and how to get it. A woman who doesn't let others dictate her worth but sets her own standards and achieves them one by one.

If you're ready to become this ultimate version of yourself, turn the page.

CHAPTER 1

THE FOUNDATIONS OF YOUR GLOW UP

Visualize the woman you want to become

This is where it all begins.

It's time to sit down and think about who you want to be. Not what your mother wants, not what your friends expect of you, not even what society pushes you to be. The person YOU want to be.

Close your eyes and visualize this woman.
Who is she?

Imagine her right down to the finest details.

What does she look like? Is she confident, bold and determined? Or calm, thoughtful and perseverant? What are her habits? What are her values?

What is her style? How does she comport herself? How does she speak? How does she interact with others? What does her social circle look like?

Think about her passions. What makes her heart race? Is it art, music, sports, cooking? What is she so passionate about that she devotes all her free time to it? What is her job? How much money is in her bank account?

Even imagine where she lives. Is it in a city-center apartment? Or in a cozy little house in the countryside? In which country?

That woman you just imagined, that's you. She is the ultimate version of yourself. The one who can achieve everything she desires.

There are no more "maybes," no more "one day." It starts today.
Right now.

Describe this woman in detail on this page.
This is the first step towards your ultimate glow up.

_____
_____
_____
_____
_____
_____
_____
_____
_____
_____
_____
_____
_____
_____
_____
_____
_____
_____
_____
_____
_____
_____
_____
_____
_____

THOUGHT OF THE DAY

"The only person you are destined to become is the person you decide to be."
Ralph Waldo Emerson

— Adopt the mindset of this woman at every moment —

Now that you have identified this ultimate version of yourself, you must make sure to adopt her mindset at every moment of your life.

This means you need to **live, think, and act like the person you want to be**. For every action, every choice, every decision you make, you must ask yourself:
"Would this person act this way?"

For example, if you have decided that the ultimate version of yourself is a successful woman in her career, then you behave as such. You don't get distracted by excuses or temptations. You do what is necessary, even if it requires sacrifices.

And if you feel the urge to procrastinate, ask yourself: "Would this person procrastinate?" Since you know the answer is no, you do what needs to be done even if you don't feel like it, because that's what this person would do.

If you want to become a confident woman ready to do anything to achieve her goals but find yourself paralyzed by the fear of failure, ask yourself: "Would this self-assured woman doubt herself?" No, she would trust herself and not let the fear of failure stop her from moving forward.

If you have decided that the person you wish to be is a fit and athletic woman, you adopt her habits. You get up early to exercise. You eat healthily, even when you feel like indulging in sweets.

In summary, adopting the mindset of the woman you have described means living your life in alignment with this vision at all times.

Harness the power of the Law of Attraction

Now we're going to discuss a powerful tool that will literally transform your life: the Law of Attraction.

The Law of Attraction is an incredibly powerful principle that governs our reality. Simply put, it states that **you attract into your life whatever you focus on**. If your thoughts are predominantly negative, you will attract more negativity. Conversely, if you focus on the positive, you will attract positivity.

Imagine yourself as a giant magnet. What you emit—whether thoughts, emotions, or desires—comes back to you as tangible reality. It's like sending a request to the universe, and it returns to you in a perfectly wrapped package.

If you spend your days telling yourself that you're not good enough and that you'll never achieve your goals, you trap yourself in a cycle of negative thoughts that impact your real life. On the other hand, if you focus on positive thoughts and visualize your successes, you create positive energy that draws you toward those successes.

Let's say you want to become an entrepreneur. If you only dream about it while watching others succeed, nothing will happen. But if you focus on this goal and truly believe in it, you'll start to act differently without even realizing it. And that's where the magic happens. You'll open yourself to the opportunities that come your way and notice paths you would have otherwise overlooked. Gradually, you'll get closer to your goal.

The key is to master your thoughts and emotions to intentionally direct your mind toward what you want in life.

The Law of Attraction in action:

When you focus your mind on a specific goal, you program your subconscious to look for ways to achieve that goal.

— Use the Law of Attraction to get what you desire —

Now, let's explore how to harness the power of the Law of Attraction to obtain what you desire in your life.

Step 1: Be clear about what you want

Take time to think about what you want to attract into your life. Whether it's a new job, a romantic relationship, or your dream house, define exactly what you want and be as specific as possible. The clearer you are about your desires, the easier it will be to attract them.

Step 2: Visualize what you want as if you already have it

Close your eyes and imagine yourself already living that reality. Feel the emotions, sensations, and experiences as if they are already happening. If you want that dream job, picture yourself working in that office with amazing colleagues. If it's a relationship you desire, imagine yourself sharing wonderful moments with that person.

Step 3: Take action

The Law of Attraction doesn't work without action. If you want that job, update your resume, send out applications, and contact recruiters. If you want that relationship, go out, meet new people, and be open to opportunities. By acting according to your desires, you send a clear message to the universe that you are ready to receive what you want.

Step 4: Let go

This might seem counterintuitive, but letting go is crucial to allowing your desires to manifest. After doing everything you can, trust the universe to guide you towards what is meant for you. Be open to signs and opportunities that come your way. Sometimes, what you receive may be even better than what you imagined.

— Why the Law of Attraction isn't working for you —

There are 5 likely reasons why the Law of Attraction doesn't seem to work for you:

Reason #1: The Law of Attraction is not an instant miracle

It doesn't work like magic by snapping your fingers. You can't just sit on the couch, briefly visualize your desires, and see them materialize in front of you in 10 minutes.

Reason #2: You lack clarity in your desires

Maybe you're not specific enough about what you want to attract, or you keep changing your mind. In this case, your energy is scattered, and you send confusing signals to the universe. It can't give you what you want if you're not sure of it yourself.

Reason #3: You lack conviction

If you constantly doubt that the Law of Attraction works for you, it won't work. Your skeptical attitude acts as a block that prevents the Universe from giving you what you desire. If you want it to work, you absolutely need to believe in it 100%.

Reason #4: You don't take action

Perhaps you visualize and feel your emotions, but you don't take action. If you remain passive, nothing will happen. So instead of just waiting for things to happen, take charge of your life and move towards your goals.

Reason #5: You are too negative

If you spend your time complaining and focusing on what's wrong in your life, you attract more negativity. Remember: you attract what you focus upon.

The Law of Attraction is...

The Universe is always conspiring in your favor.
Things happen for you, not against you.
What you desire will be given to you at the right moment.
Trust the timing of the Universe.

— Turn your dreams into reality through manifestation —

Manifestation goes beyond the Law of Attraction. It's the art of transforming your thoughts into tangible reality through specific actions.

There are several manifestation techniques you can use to create the life of your dreams:

1. Creative visualization

As we discussed earlier, creative visualization is one of the crucial steps to using the Law of Attraction to your advantage. It's the **most powerful manifestation method to bring your dreams to life**.

Visualization involves vividly and emotionally imagining the fulfillment of your desires. It's more than just "thinking" about what you want. It's like creating a movie in your mind where you are the main character and your dreams unfold before your eyes.

Why is this so powerful? Because **your subconscious cannot distinguish between what you imagine and reality**. By visualizing regularly and intensely, you program your mind to believe that these desires are already fulfilled. And once your mind is convinced, the universe follows.

When you visualize, use all your senses to make the visualization even more powerful. See the vibrant colors, hear the sounds, smell the scents, feel the textures. The more vivid your visualization, the more effective it will be.

And remember consistency. Make visualization a daily habit. The more you practice, the stronger your belief that your desires are already fulfilled. And the more convinced you become, the more you will attract what you desire.

2. Vision boards

A vision board is a **visualization tool where you display images, words, and affirmations that represent your goals and desires**. It's like a collage of everything that constitutes your dream life and what you want to attract to yourself.

Creating your vision board is very simple. You can use a piece of poster board if you want a physical board, or an application like Canva to create a digital vision board.

Next, find images that illustrate your desires, inspirational quotes, and keywords that motivate you. You can cut out pictures from magazines, print images from the internet, or simply find inspiration on Pinterest. Include everything that represents your deepest dreams, whether it's images of places you want to travel, your dream house, or the romantic relationship you wish to have.

Once you have gathered all these elements, arrange them on your vision board in a way that constantly reminds you of your goals.

The secret to an effective vision board is to look at it every day. Place it somewhere you will see it regularly, whether on your wall, on your desk, or even as a wallpaper on your phone. Each time you look at it, visualize your desires as if they have already become true.

3. Positive affirmations

You can use positive affirmations to reinforce your thoughts and beliefs related to your goals. For example, if you want to attract money into your life, repeat phrases like "I deserve financial abundance" or "I am wealthy" to reprogram your mind towards success. Repeat them daily with conviction and determination, sincerely believing in them. We will explore the power of positive affirmations in more detail in the chapter on self-confidence and self-love.

4. Journaling

You can also keep a manifestation journal where you write down your goals and intentions every day to manifest the life of your dreams.

One of the most well-known journaling techniques in manifestation is the 369 method: write your goal 3 times in the morning, 6 times in the afternoon, and 9 times in the evening, for 33 to 45 days.

— To get what you want, you must let go —

The ultimate secret to manifesting what you want in life is the **Law of Detachment**. It might seem paradoxical, but if you want something desperately, you need some emotional detachment in order to obtain it. Let me explain.

Essentially, it means **detaching from the final outcome while putting all your energy into achieving your goals**. You focus on what you can control—your actions and mindset—rather than desperately clinging to a specific result. Trust that what you want will come to you at the right time, and don't let obstacles or delays unsettle you.

From a spiritual perspective, it's important to acknowledge that you don't have total control over the events in your life and trusting the universe's plan, even if you don't always understand it. We often think we can plan and control everything in our lives. But the truth is, the universe's plan for us is sometimes much better than what we could have imagined.

Let me give you a concrete example: imagine you have a job interview for your dream job. Instead of worrying about whether you'll get the job or not, focus on what you can control. Practice talking about your previous experiences, research the company, and prepare for the interview as best as you can.

Once you've done everything you can, let go. Tell yourself that if you've done everything within your power, the universe will take care of the rest. Detach yourself from the obsessive need to have this job. If you get it, great. If not, believe that this job wasn't meant for you and that if you had gotten it, you might have realized after some time that it wasn't the right position for you.

— Your thoughts determine the course of your life —

You need to understand that **your life will always head in the direction of your dominant thoughts**, those that are the strongest, because they have the most influence on your actions and outcomes.

Positive and optimistic thoughts are like seeds you plant in your mind. The more you nurture them, the more they grow and flourish in your life. By cultivating these thoughts, you create a mental environment that is conducive to success, fulfillment, and happiness.

On the other hand, limiting thoughts are like weeds that stifle your growth. They tell you that you're not good enough, that you don't deserve success, that you're doomed to fail. If you let them proliferate, they will eventually choke your dreams and aspirations.

This is why you must closely monitor your thoughts. At every moment, ask yourself if your thought is bringing you closer to or further from your goals. If it's a limiting thought, replace it immediately with a positive and constructive one.

Always remember that you have the absolute power to choose your thoughts. And what you choose to think determines the quality of your life. Taking control of your mind means taking control of your life.

Take responsibility for your life

Taking responsibility for your life means recognizing that **you are the only person who has the power to change things in your life**. It means you cannot blame others, circumstances, or luck for your failures or successes. Every decision you make, every action you take, has a direct impact on your life.

If you find yourself in a difficult situation, instead of making excuses or blaming others, ask yourself what you can do to improve things. Maybe you need to change your way of thinking, make bolder decisions, or act with more determination. Whatever the case, the responsibility lies with you.

In fact, you are even 100% responsible for everything that happens to you in life.

This does not mean that everything that happens to you is your fault- far from it. There are always things beyond your control. But even in those situations, you always have control over how you react. You can choose to be overwhelmed by challenges, or you can choose to overcome them with strength and resilience.

When you take responsibility for your life, you admit that you have full control over your actions, choices, and outcomes. You acknowledge that you are not a powerless victim of circumstances. You are a creator, capable of shaping your reality according to your desires and aspirations. You stop waiting for things to change on their own or for someone else to come and save you.

No matter where you come from or what has happened in the past, you always have the choice to decide who you want to be and what you want to achieve. It's up to you to take the reins, carve out your own path, and create the life you deserve.

— Get rid of your victim mentality —

If you often say things like:

"I never have any luck,"
"Life is unfair,"
"Why does this always happen to me?"
"Nothing ever works out for me," or
"It's not my fault,"

you see yourself as powerless in the face of life's events. You have a victim mentality.

When you see yourself as a victim, you put yourself in a position of weakness. You give power to external factors, which robs you of your ability to act and change your situation. You condemn yourself to passively endure your life instead of shaping it according to your desires.

It's time to change that.

To free yourself from this toxic mentality, start by **becoming aware of your thoughts and words**. When they are negative, replace them with positive affirmations or solutions. For example, instead of saying, "Why does this always happen to me?" say, "I am capable of overcoming this challenge and coming out stronger."

Next, **focus on the actions you can take to change your situation**. Instead of dwelling on what's wrong, concentrate on what you can do to improve things. For example, when you feel like complaining, "Everyone is always criticizing me," ask yourself what you can do to develop your self-confidence and feel better about yourself.

— Stop being a spectator, become the leading actress in your life —

It's time for you to stop being a mere spectator of your own life and become the leading actress.

Being a spectator is like sitting in a cinema, passively watching the story of your life unfold before your eyes without intervening. You let circumstances carry you away and don't make the decisions that could shape your destiny. In essence, you just go with the flow of events, regardless of whether they lead you where you want to go or not.

When you are the leading actress of your life, you take control of your own script and actively decide the direction you want to take. You are proactive, determined, and make bold decisions to shape your life on your own terms.

Now that you understand the difference between these two roles, let's see how you can become the leading actress of your life:

1. **Take Control:** Stop letting circumstances or others decide for you. You are the only person who can truly define your destiny.

2. **Set Clear Goals**: Identify what you want to achieve in all aspects of your life, whether it's your career, relationships, or health. Clear goals will give you direction and motivate you to take action.

3. **Act with Determination and Proactivity**: Don't let fear or uncertainty hold you back. Dare to step out of your comfort zone, take calculated risks, and move confidently toward your goals. Remember that every small step counts.

— No one can save you but yourself —

You may have an incredible partner, a circle of friends, and family who are there for you, but ultimately, it's you who makes the decisions. It's you who gets up every morning and decides how to approach your day. It's you who chooses your actions, reactions, goals, and priorities.

Others can offer advice and encouragement, but they cannot live your life for you. They can't make the tough choices for you. They can't overcome obstacles on your behalf.

No one knows better than you what you need, what you truly want, and where you want to go. No one can change your life for you. This may seem intimidating, but it is also liberating because it means you are not limited by the expectations, opinions, or judgments of others. You are free to follow your own path and shape your future.

When you accept this responsibility, something magical happens. You become stronger, more resilient, more confident. You realize that you are capable of overcoming anything, that you have within you all the resources needed to succeed.

So take the reins of your life. Set ambitious goals and work tirelessly to achieve them. Don't wait for conditions to be perfect, because they never will be. Be the source of your own inspiration. Believe in yourself and your abilities. Start now, with what you have and where you are. And never stop fighting for what you want.

CHAPTER 2

MANAGING YOUR EMOTIONS

If you truly want to reach this higher version of yourself, you absolutely must learn to **master your emotions**. It's non-negotiable. If you don't control them, they will control you.

Let me give you a concrete example. Imagine you're having a wonderful day, everything is going perfectly, and then suddenly, someone makes a small remark. Maybe they criticize your work or the way you dress.

If you let this remark upset you, your entire day is ruined. You feel hurt, frustrated, angry. You find yourself dwelling on the critique, wondering if you're really good enough, and before you know it, you're overwhelmed by doubt and insecurity.

This is where you need to understand the importance of mastering your emotions. If you had learned to take a step back, to put things in perspective, and not let others' words have such power over you, you could continue your day as if nothing happened.

Now, imagine another situation. This time, you receive the same remark, but instead of being carried away by your emotions, you remain calm, confident, and unshaken. You know who you are and what you're worth, and you refuse to let others' opinions unsettle you.

That's what managing your emotions is about. It's about taking control of your own life, instead of letting others do it for you. It's freeing yourself from the grip of stress, anxiety, and fear, so you can move forward with confidence and assurance.

You need to learn to understand your emotions, dominate them, and use them to your advantage. If you let them take over, they can lead you to make impulsive decisions or act irrationally. You really cannot neglect this aspect of your glow up, it's extremely important.

Never let others influence your inner peace

There's something fundamental you need to understand: people will ***always*** have something to say. Whether it's criticisms, judgments, or opinions you don't want to hear, it will never stop.

Now, think about all those times you let someone's hurtful comments haunt you for days, even weeks. Why did you allow them to affect you in such a way? Why did you give them that power? It's time to take back control. This is your life. You are in the driver's seat. You have absolute control over your inner peace, and no one should have the power to take it away from you.

You need to learn to filter what you let enter your mind. If someone says something hurtful, ask yourself:

Is it really worth letting this affect me?
Does this person truly deserve the power to ruin my day?

The answer is probably no.

No one should have the power to influence how you feel, think, or live. So, when someone tries to make you doubt yourself, to make you feel less than you are, simply remind yourself of who you really are. You can choose to let others' words hurt and disturb you, or you can choose to step back and not let them affect you. It might seem difficult at first, but with a bit of practice, it will become second nature.

Stop trying to control everything

You need to hear this:

Stop wasting your energy trying to control everything that happens around you. It will lead you nowhere.

Let me give you a simple example- the weather. You cannot control whether tomorrow will be sunny or rainy. No matter how much you want a sunny day for your perfect beach outing, you can't command the sun to shine or the clouds to disappear.

And what about the people around you? You cannot control their actions, thoughts, or feelings. You can give them your best, be there for them, but ultimately, it's up to them to decide their behavior. You can positively influence them, but you can't dictate their actions. Accept it. It's liberating, trust me.

How many times have you found yourself agonizing, biting your nails, letting anxiety consume you because you were desperately trying to control situations that were simply beyond your grasp? You spend hours worrying about things that are not under your control, and this obsession keeps you in a state of constant stress, frustration, and disappointment.

You need to accept that some things in life are simply beyond your control.

Remember this rule:
If you can't control it, don't worry about it.

— You can't control everything that happens to you, but you can control how you react —

You can be the most prepared, organized person in the world, but there will always be things beyond your control that come out of nowhere. You can't change them since you don't have control over them. But the good news is, **you decide how you react to these events**. And believe me, that's where your true power lies.

Start by stopping the complaints. Yes, it's tempting to think that the world is unfair and that everything is doomed, but that won't change anything. Instead of dwelling on your misfortunes, try to take control of yourself.

How you react to what happens to you is your superpower. Imagine it like a video game. You can't always control the progression of the game, but you can control the movements of your character. And it's the same in life. You can choose how you react to obstacles, challenges, and unexpected situations. You can choose to be defeated or to rise stronger than ever. Don't let fear, anger, or despair destabilize you.

So how do you master this superpower? First, take a pause. Breathe deeply. Don't react immediately. Give yourself time to digest what just happened. Then, evaluate the situation objectively and think about your options.

Ask yourself:
"What do I do now to handle this?"

Next, take control of your thoughts. Remember, you have the power to choose what you focus on. Instead of being carried away by negative or destructive thoughts, train yourself to see the positive side, find solutions, and focus on what you can learn from the situation.

THOUGHT OF THE DAY

"Life is 10% what happens to us and 90% how we react to it."
Charles R. Swindoll

— 6 strategies to learn to let go —

Here are 6 concrete strategies you can implement right now to help you let go.

1. Identify What Is Beyond Your Control

Take a sheet of paper and list everything that worries you at the moment. Then, divide this list into two columns: what you can control and what is beyond your control. Focus only on the first column and look for solutions.

2. Imagine the Worst-Case Scenario

When you start stressing about a situation, try to imagine the worst thing that could happen and whether you could survive it. Often, you'll realize that it's not really the end of the world.

3. Take a Step Back in Time

Ask yourself: "Will this situation really matter in 5 years?" If not, don't spend more than 5 minutes worrying about it.

4. Accept Imperfection

You're going to make mistakes; it's inevitable. But instead of letting them get you down, accept them as opportunities to learn and grow. No one is perfect. What matters is that you get up every time and keep moving forward.

5. Develop a Relaxation Routine

Incorporate relaxing activities into your daily life, such as meditation, yoga, or reading. These moments of relaxation will help you release pressure and recharge your batteries.

6. Practice Gratitude

Every day, take time to be grateful for what you have in your life. Focus on the positive aspects rather than getting absorbed by problems.

You are not responsible for others' emotions

How many times have you felt guilty for something that shouldn't make you feel guilty?

You are a person with your own feelings, goals, and challenges, and the same goes for others. Their emotions, reactions, happiness, or sadness—all of that belongs to them. It doesn't belong to you. You don't have the power to control how others feel, and that's perfectly normal.

Imagine your best friend asks you to accompany her to a party, and you say no. She gets angry and tells you she's really disappointed that you're letting her go alone. What happens in your mind? You start to feel bad, want to justify yourself, and question your decision. But is it really your fault that she reacted the way she did? Of course not. **It's your right to say no when you need to, without feeling responsible for others' reactions**. It's *her* responsibility to manage her emotions.

Now, imagine you want to become an entrepreneur, but your family thinks you should have a more stable, traditional job. If you feel responsible for their frustration, you might hold yourself back from pursuing your dreams, even if it makes you unhappy. But **when you realize that their emotions are not your responsibility, you free yourself to live your life as you see fit**.

You have the right to be yourself and live for yourself, even if it bothers those around you. Others' emotions are the result of their own experiences, beliefs, and perceptions of the world. You can't control that.

This doesn't mean you should be insensitive to others' emotions. On the contrary, you can show empathy while maintaining your boundaries. For example, if someone blames you for something that isn't your responsibility, you can listen to what they have to say, but you don't have to absorb their emotions.

Never take things personally

If you've read *"The Four Agreements"* by Don Miguel Ruiz, you're probably already familiar with this concept.

Here are some signs that indicate you tend to take things personally:

1. **You often interpret others' actions or words as specifically directed at you even when it's not the case** (for example, if someone is in a bad mood, you immediately think it's because of something you did).

2. **You react immediately with strong negative emotions** like anger, sadness, or frustration when someone criticizes you.

3. **You frequently doubt your own value or abilities after receiving negative feedback or comments**.

4. **You replay negative comments over and over in your mind**, wondering why they were directed at you.

5. **You feel personally attacked every time you receive feedback**, even when it's constructive.

The truth is, most of the time, the negative criticisms you receive reveal more about the person giving them than they do about you.

For example, imagine a colleague who constantly criticizes your physical appearance. You might think it's because you're not attractive enough or not dressed well enough. But in reality, it could simply reflect her own discomfort with her appearance.

Now, suppose you've decided to change careers and you tell a close friend. You've thought through every detail and are super excited about this new chapter in your life. Instead of hearing, "Wow, it's amazing that you've decided to take control of your life, I'm so proud of you!", she says, "Hmm, are you sure that's a good idea? It's really risky, don't you think?" Know that this has absolutely nothing to do with you. She's simply projecting her own fear of failure onto you.

Keep in mind that others' words are merely a reflection of their own insecurities and frustrations.

If someone criticizes you, instead of letting it bring you down, show them compassion. Think about what they must be feeling deep inside to feel the need to put you down. And most importantly, remember that their words can only hurt you if you allow them to.

The Law of the Mirror

A person often criticizes in others what they refuse to see in themselves.

Learn to manage your stress and anxiety

Stress and anxiety are silent killers that can sabotage you without you even realizing it, slowing down your progress towards your glow up. You need to be extremely attentive to the signals your body and mind are sending you.

Here are the signs that you might be suffering from anxiety without knowing it:

- You struggle to focus on one thing at a time.

- You become irritable or defensive even in normally low-stress situations.

- You often wake up feeling tired, even after a good night's sleep.

- You have difficulty falling asleep, staying asleep, or you have frequent nightmares.

- You spend a lot of time worrying about things that might happen or thinking about the worst-case scenario.

- Your muscles are tense, especially in the shoulders, neck, and back, even without engaging in intense physical activity.

Later on, we will explore techniques you can incorporate into your daily routine to manage your stress and anxiety effectively.

— Cognitive distortions that worsen your anxiety —

Cognitive distortions are **automatic, thoughtless patterns that lead you to interpret situations incorrectly and negatively**. They make you see the world through a distorted lens, causing you to doubt yourself, your abilities, and even your worth as a person. By becoming aware of these cognitive distortions, you can counter them and take control of your mind.

Here are the most common cognitive distortions related to anxiety:

All-or-Nothing Thinking: You see situations as all-or-nothing, black or white, never or always, with no middle ground. For example, you might think, "If I fail this job interview, I am a total failure."

Catastrophizing: You imagine the worst possible scenario and consider it inevitable. For example, "If I don't succeed in this presentation, my career is over."

Selective Abstraction: You focus solely on the negative aspects of a situation while ignoring the positive ones. For example, you might dwell on one negative comment despite receiving numerous compliments.

Personalization: You take responsibility for situations that are out of your control. For example, "It's my fault that my friend is in a bad mood."

Arbitrary Inferences: You draw conclusions without sufficient evidence to support them. For example, "My boss didn't say hello this morning, so they must hate me."

Overgeneralization: You take a single negative experience and generalize it to all situations. For example, if you fail an exam, you might think, "I'm terrible at everything I do."

Exaggeration: You amplify the negative aspects of a situation and make them more significant than they actually are. For example, if you make a small mistake at work, you might think it's a disaster and everyone will find you ridiculous.

Disqualifying the Positive: You systematically reject or minimize the positive aspects of your life or yourself. For example, if someone compliments your work, you might think, "They're just saying that to be nice."

Emotional Reasoning: You let your emotions dictate your perception of reality, rather than basing your thoughts on objective facts. For example, if you feel rejected by a friend, you might believe that everyone dislikes you.

Faulty Reasoning: You use unsound arguments to justify your thoughts or actions. For example, "I can't succeed in this project because I've never been good at this."

Labeling: You define yourself or others by a single characteristic or action, ignoring the complexity of the person or situation. If you make a mistake, you might think, "I am completely useless" instead of "I made a mistake."

False Obligations: These are arbitrary rules you impose on yourself or accept as immutable truths, even if they aren't based on reality or your own values. For example, "I must always be nice to everyone, even if it means putting them before myself."

When you are aware of these cognitive distortions, you can step back from the negative thoughts causing you anxiety and examine them objectively.

To identify cognitive distortions in your thoughts, you can ask yourself these questions:

- Am I jumping to negative conclusions without concrete evidence?

- Am I focusing only on the negative aspects of a situation while ignoring the positive ones?

- Am I overgeneralizing based on a single negative experience?

- Am I viewing things in extreme, all-or-nothing terms?

- Am I turning a small worry into a monumental catastrophe?

- Am I criticizing or judging myself harshly without acknowledging my successes or strengths?

- Am I making negative predictions about the future without considering positive possibilities?

- Am I engaging in self-sabotage due to fear of failure or judgment from others?

- Are my emotions overwhelming my ability to reason objectively?

By replacing your distorted thoughts with more realistic and constructive ones, you will change the way you perceive yourself and interpret the world around you.

— 6 effective relaxation techniques to relieve stress and anxiety —

Here are methods that can help you manage your anxiety:

1. The 5-4-3-2-1 technique

This method helps you refocus your attention on the present moment, setting aside the anxious thoughts that overwhelm you. It involves identifying and concentrating on:

- 5 things you can see (a carpet, a wall, ...)
- 4 things you can hear (the sound of cars, the wind, ...)
- 3 things you can touch (your skin, a piece of clothing, ...)
- 2 things you can smell (a perfume, spices, ...)
- 1 thing you can taste (a drink, a fruit, ...)

It's a simple but incredibly effective technique to break the cycle of anxiety.

2. Heart coherence

Heart coherence is a breathing technique that allows you to synchronize the rhythm of your heart with your breathing to create a state of deep calm.

Here's how it works: **take a deep breath in for 5 seconds**, then **exhale for 5 seconds. Repeat this for 5 minutes**.

It might seem too simple to be effective, but trust me, it works. Studies have shown that heart coherence can reduce your stress levels, improve your concentration, and even boost your immune system.

You can practice heart coherence anytime you feel tense, stressed, or anxious.

3. Journaling

Journaling is like having a conversation with yourself, but on paper. During the process you ask yourself questions, let your thoughts flow freely, and write down whatever comes to mind. No filters, no judgments. Just you and your thoughts. When you take the time to put these thoughts on paper, you externalize them. You give them a tangible form. And once they're there in front of you, you can start to understand and tame them.

So, the first step is to **write down all the thoughts looping in your head and your current emotions**. Let everything out. Express your fear, frustration, anger, whatever you're feeling. Then, dig a little deeper.

Ask yourself why these thoughts are troubling you so much. What triggers them? Are there recurring patterns in your thinking? Are they based on facts? Or are they products of your imagination? Try to question them.

4. Gratitude

When you feel anxious or stressed, **focus on what you're grateful for**. It can be anything. Maybe you managed to get a good night's sleep. Or perhaps the sun is shining outside. Or just the fact that you're breathing. Whatever it is, take the time to truly feel it.

It's not a magical solution that will instantly save you from anxiety, but when you focus on what you're grateful for, it changes your perspective. It reminds you that there is always something positive, even in difficult times. That gives you control over your own mind. Instead of letting anxiety overwhelm you, you tell your brain, "No, today we're focusing on the positive things in my life."

5. Physical activity

You don't need to engage in intense workout sessions to feel better. Just moving your body is enough to release endorphins— happy hormones. Walk, dance, do yoga, Pilates, whatever you prefer. The important thing is to release that stressful energy building up inside you.

6. Mindfulness meditation

Mindfulness meditation is a technique that allows you to anchor yourself in the present moment without any judgment. You focus on what you feel, your breathing, and the sensations in your body. It's like pressing the "pause" button and recentering on yourself.

When you feel overwhelmed by anxiety, find a quiet place. Sit comfortably, close your eyes, and focus on your breathing. Inhale. Exhale. Feel the air entering and leaving your nostrils, how your belly rises and falls. Let your thoughts wander freely, but observe them as if you were watching clouds pass in the sky. You don't need to hold onto them or analyze them. They come, and then they go. Bring your attention back to the present moment by focusing on your bodily sensations. You can feel your feet on the ground, the warmth of your hands, or even the weight of your body on the chair. This brings you back to the present moment, where anxiety has no power. When you feel ready to end your meditation, take a few deep breaths and slowly open your eyes.

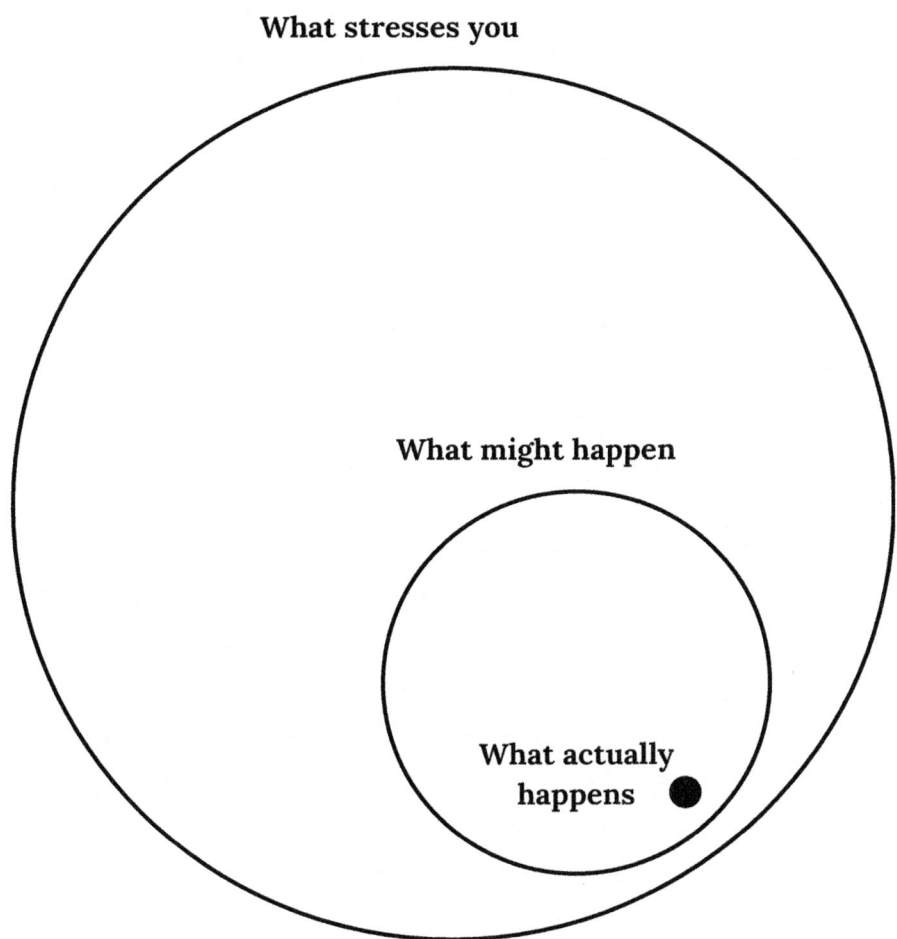

CHAPTER 3

BOOSTING YOUR SELF-CONFIDENCE AND SELF-LOVE

If you've enjoyed this book so far, I would really appreciate it if you could leave a quick review on Amazon.

It takes less than a minute, but it would greatly help me get my work known and reach other ambitious women.

Just scan this QR code with your phone

Thank you so much for your support; it means a lot to me.
Now, let's get back to business.

It's time to recognize your worth

I'm going to start by telling you something crucial: you won't be able to glow up until you recognize your own worth.

So, I want you to take a few minutes to make a list of all the things that make you an exceptional person on the next page.

To help you write this list, ask yourself these questions:

What do you love about yourself?

What are your strengths and qualities?

What have you accomplished in your life that you are truly proud of?

What makes you feel good about yourself?

What impresses people about you?

What compliments do you often receive?

What challenges have you successfully overcome in your life?

In what areas are you skilled and confident?

What makes you unique compared to others?

Once your list is complete, I want you to read it once a day. In the morning when you wake up, or in the evening before you go to bed, it doesn't matter. The goal is to immerse yourself in these words to change your perspective on yourself and boost your self-confidence.

I am an incredible woman because...

— Learn to accept and savor a compliment —

There's a fundamental skill you absolutely need to master: the art of accepting a compliment.

It might seem simple, but I assure you it's not as easy as it sounds.

Why is it so important? Because when you reject a compliment, you're sending a message to your brain that you don't deserve that recognition. Your brain will listen and internalize that message. And over time, by refusing compliments, you slowly destroy your own self-esteem.

Now, let's look at the **three wrong ways to react when someone compliments you**:

The first is **deflection**. This is when you avoid or downplay the compliment. For example, if someone says your presentation was amazing, and you respond with, "Oh, it was nothing, anyone could have done it." No, you're wrong. You did a great job, so accept it.

Next is **reciprocity**. This is when you feel obliged to return the compliment immediately. For example, if someone tells you that you look beautiful in that dress, and you reply, "Thank you, you look beautiful too." Stop that. Simply accept the compliment without feeling the need to return it right away.

The third is **self-deprecation**. This is when you put yourself down after receiving a compliment. For example, someone compliments your cooking skills, and you respond with, "Oh, but I burned the dessert yesterday." No, stop. Focus on the compliment and leave the self-criticism aside for once.

Here's the **golden rule: when someone compliments you, just say "thank you."** No justifications, no downplaying, no returning the compliment. The more you accept compliments, the better you'll feel about yourself. It's like a virtuous circle.

Reprogram your subconscious mind

Your subconscious is that part of your mind that operates in the background, automatically and without your conscious awareness. It stores all your beliefs, habits, memories, fears, desires, and perceptions.

Now, you need to know this:
Your life is 95% driven by this subconscious.

This means that most of your choices, actions, and reactions are dictated by this part of you that you don't consciously control.

Think about it for a moment. Do you wonder why you always react the same way to certain situations? It's your subconscious taking over. Do you find it hard to change certain habits? It's your subconscious holding you back.

Let's imagine you want to lose weight, for example. Your conscious mind might be super motivated, determined to follow a strict diet and exercise regularly. But if your subconscious isn't on board, you'll never reach your goal.

Your subconscious has a huge impact on your glow up.

In this section, we will explore how to reprogram your subconscious so it works in your favor and helps you become the best version of yourself.

— The impact of limiting beliefs on your life —

A limiting belief is something you believe to be true about yourself, others, or the world around you, and it holds you back from progressing toward your ultimate version.

Your limiting beliefs can form in various ways. Sometimes they are passed down by your family, friends, or other influential people in your life. For example, if your parents constantly criticize you for everything, you might develop the belief that you are never good enough, no matter what you do.

These beliefs can also stem from past experiences or repetitive thoughts. Perhaps you had a job interview that went very badly, and now you think you are destined to fail all job interviews forever: that's a limiting belief.

These beliefs **are not actual facts**. They are thoughts you have accepted as true, but they are not necessarily so. And the worst part is, the more you believe them, the more you behave as if they were a reality.

Here are other examples of limiting beliefs:

I am incapable of speaking in public
He will never love me because I'm not beautiful enough
I don't have enough experience to apply for this job
I'm too shy for anyone to be interested in me
I will never succeed
Others are better than me
It's too late to change my life
I'm not lucky

The good news is that you can change these beliefs. But to do that, you must start by identifying them. That's what we will explore on the next page.

— Becoming aware of your limiting beliefs —

To identify your main limiting beliefs, you can start by pinpointing the situations that are holding you back and that you really want to change.

Write them down below, starting with "I want...".

For example:

"I want to get this job"
"I want to lose weight"
"I want to find love"
"I want to become a charismatic woman"

Now, place one or more "but" after each sentence you just wrote and list all the reasons why you think you can't achieve it.

For example:

"I want to get this job *but I'm not smart enough*"
"I want to lose weight *but I don't have time to exercise*"
"I want to find love *but no one will love me as I am*"
"I want to become a charismatic woman *but I'm incapable of speaking in public*"

_____
_____
_____
_____
_____
_____
_____

All these "buts" you just wrote down are your limiting beliefs.
Now, it's time to get rid of them.

— 4 techniques to overcome your limiting beliefs —

Here are four ways to free yourself from these limiting beliefs:

1. Look for contradictory evidence that proves these beliefs are false or can change

Examine your beliefs objectively and ask yourself, "Are these thoughts really true?" Are these beliefs based on concrete facts or simply on your own biased perception? For example, if you believe you are not smart enough to get your dream job, ask yourself why you believe that. What past experiences or influences have shaped this belief?

Now, look for contradictory evidence that proves these beliefs are not real. This is where you start breaking the vicious cycle of your limiting thoughts. If you think you are not smart enough, remember times when you successfully solved difficult problems at work or during your studies. If you feel that you are incapable of speaking in public, think back to moments when you managed to do it, whether during a family meeting or in a group of friends. These situations are tangible proof that your limiting beliefs are based on false ideas rather than real facts.

2. Step out of your comfort zone and take daily actions toward your goals despite your beliefs to diminish their power

Stepping out of your comfort zone is an excellent way to weaken your limiting beliefs because it exposes you to new experiences that prove these beliefs are not necessarily true.

Imagine once again that you think you are incapable of speaking in public. To step out of your comfort zone, start with small actions. For instance, you can volunteer to present a project during a team meeting or give a speech in front of a small group of friends. Each time you overcome your fear and speak in public, you weaken the power of this limiting belief a little more.

Next, set yourself more ambitious goals, such as giving a presentation in front of a larger audience. Each step you take reinforces your belief that this limiting belief is not truly grounded and that you can overcome it.

3. Visualize yourself succeeding and overcoming your limiting beliefs

Close your eyes, take a deep breath, and imagine yourself facing your fears. Visualize yourself confronting them with confidence. For example, if you are afraid of public speaking, picture yourself giving a speech with confidence. By imagining yourself succeeding, you strengthen your belief in your abilities and soften your limiting belief. The more you visualize overcoming these obstacles, the more capable you will feel of facing them in reality.

4. Automatically challenge every negative thought and replace it with a positive affirmation

We have already discussed positive affirmations several times in this book. But what exactly are they?

A positive affirmation is a short, direct statement that reinforces a positive thought. Instead of being overwhelmed by self-destructive negative beliefs, you can replace these beliefs with affirmations that boost your confidence and self-esteem. It may seem simple, but it is very powerful.

To take the previous example, as soon as you tell yourself that you are incapable of speaking in public, transform that thought into a positive affirmation like "I am capable of speaking in public with assurance and confidence." This needs to become an automatic habit for you. Immediately challenge a negative thought by replacing it with a positive affirmation.

For your positive affirmations to have a real impact, you must formulate them in a specific way:

- Phrase them in the present tense and first person "I":
Express your affirmations as if they are already a reality. For example, instead of saying "I will become more confident," say "I am confident."

- Be specific:
Clearly identify what you want to achieve or manifest. Avoid vague or general affirmations. The more specific your affirmation, the more effective it will be.

- Use positive words:
Choose positive and encouraging words that evoke feelings of confidence, success, and self-esteem. Avoid negative or restrictive terms.

You must absolutely integrate your positive affirmations into your daily routine so that they truly become a part of you. Repeat them out loud each morning while looking at yourself in the mirror. Write them on post-it notes and stick them on your mirror, desk, or fridge. Note them down in a journal and read them before going to bed. The more you see and hear them, the more deeply they will become ingrained in your mind.

— Pay attention to how you talk to yourself —

The way you talk to yourself can change everything in your life. The words you use in your inner dialogue have a real impact on your confidence, motivation, and ability to achieve your goals.

I want you to remember this:
You need to talk to yourself the way you would talk to your little sister.

If your little sister needs a boost, you wouldn't say, "You're useless, just give up." No, you would say things like, "You are amazing and you've worked hard to get here. I believe in you, everything is going to be great, you're going to crush it." And if things go wrong, you would reassure her by saying that it happens to everyone, that she did her best, and that next time will be better.

Do you see the difference?

You treat yourself more harshly than you would treat anyone else, and you say things to yourself that you would never accept from another person.

It's time to change that and start using words that build you up instead of tearing you down.

When you make a mistake, instead of telling yourself that you're worthless, tell yourself that it's an opportunity to learn, grow, and become better. When you look in the mirror, instead of criticizing yourself, find something you love about yourself.

The next time you catch yourself talking to yourself as if you were your own worst enemy, stop. Think about what you're saying and ask yourself: Would I talk to my little sister like this?

If the answer is no, change your self-talk.

Phrases you absolutely need to eliminate from your vocabulary to glow up:

"I'm definitely going to fail"
"I'm really bad at this"
"I can't do it"
"There's no point in trying, I give up"
"I'm not pretty/smart/interesting enough"
"I never have any luck"
"Others will make fun of me"
"It's impossible"
"I'm too anxious to succeed"
"I'm not the right person for this"
"I can't change who I am"

— Explore your dark side through shadow work —

Shadow work is a deep introspection process that allows you to delve into the darkest areas of your personality. These are parts of yourself that you often prefer to ignore, repress, or are not even aware of. Your fears, insecurities, self-destructive behaviors— everything that holds you back.

These parts of you have a huge impact on your life. It's like having a weight on your shoulders that you can't feel but that prevents you from moving forward. This shadow side fuels your self-sabotage, making you feel bad about yourself, underestimate your abilities, procrastinate, and put obstacles in your own path.

Here's how you can start the shadow work process:

1. Become aware of your emotions:

Find a quiet place and take a moment to listen carefully to what your body and mind are telling you. What negative emotions do you regularly feel in different situations in your life? Is it anger that rises when someone upsets you? Or maybe sadness that surfaces when you feel lonely? Perhaps you feel fear in certain circumstances?

Take a pen and a journal, and write down these emotions. Simply putting words to your feelings will help you understand and start to manage them. The goal here is not to judge these emotions as good or bad, but simply to recognize and accept them as part of you.

Become aware of how these emotions physically manifest in your body. Is it a knot in your stomach, tension in your shoulders, or something else? The more aware you are of these signals, the better you will be able to understand and transform them.

2. Identify your triggers:

Now, delve a bit deeper into your experiences. What events, situations, or even people trigger these emotions in you? Look for recurring patterns. Perhaps there are certain interactions with family members or colleagues that consistently make you angry. Or maybe there are certain memories that evoke deep sadness. Take the time to identify these triggers. The goal is to understand what lies behind these emotional reactions.

3. Ask yourself the right questions:

After identifying your emotions and their triggers, try to understand the roots of these emotions by asking yourself the right questions.

For example, if you feel anger every time you are criticized at work, reflect upon why this criticism affects you so much. What are you afraid of losing? Is there a past wound that gets reactivated in these moments? Be honest with yourself, even if it's difficult. These questions can help you identify the thought patterns or the limiting beliefs that fuel your emotions.

4. Write down your thoughts:

The act of writing is incredibly powerful in this process. It allows you to clarify your thoughts and release the emotional energy that may be blocked inside you. When exploring your emotions and thoughts, take the time to write them down in your journal. Write everything that comes to mind, without censoring yourself. Unleash all your thoughts, fears, and resentments onto the paper. Don't hold back. Let it all out.

Shadow work is a complex process, and I strongly encourage you to explore it in depth on your own to reap all its benefits.

Live for yourself, not for others

— Don't let others' opinions dictate your life —

If you spend your life worrying about what others think of you, you will never truly live your own life.

People will always have something to say. They think they know what's best for you and will tell you what you should do, what you should wear, how you should act. And the worst part is, they don't really know you. Their perception of you is colored by their own filters and judgments. That's why the only thing that matters is what you think of yourself.

Having confidence in yourself means believing in yourself— regardless of what others think of you. It's recognizing your own worth, strengths, and abilities without needing anyone's approval. This is the level of self-confidence you should strive to achieve and if you believe in yourself— if you trust your choices and actions— then no one can stop you.

Here are my four tips to help you detach from others' opinions:

1. Get to know yourself and fully accept yourself. The more you are in tune with yourself, the less sensitive you will be to judgments.

2. Distance yourself from others' opinions. Ask yourself this question: "Will this person's opinion really impact my life in 5 years?" The answer is probably no.

3. Remember that you can't please everyone. You are not here to meet everyone's expectations.

4. Surround yourself with supportive and encouraging people. Your social circle plays a crucial role in your self-confidence and your ability to detach from others' opinions. Choose friends and loved ones who believe in you and inspire you to be the best version of yourself.

— Stop wasting your time trying to impress people —

I have a little thought exercise for you: think of three people, whether you know them personally or not, who are truly successful in life. Take the time to visualize them clearly.

Got it?

Now, ask yourself this question: are these three people successful because they conform to others' expectations, or because they stay true to themselves regardless of what others think? I'm sure you know the answer.

The truth is, you will never thrive and become the ultimate version of yourself if you spend your time trying to become what others want you to be. Life is far too short to pretend to be someone you're not. Every second you spend trying to please everyone is a second you can never get back. And believe me, you don't want to look back and realize you wasted years playing a role that wasn't yours.

You know what's truly impressive? Having the courage to be authentic, to follow your own path, no matter what others think. That's what attracts the right people into your life, those who love and respect you for who you truly are.

What really matters is being yourself, without compromise. That's what will make you truly fulfilled and accomplished. You don't need others' approval to validate your worth. The only approval you need is your own.

So, the next time you find yourself trying to impress someone, ask yourself if it's really worth it and if it brings you closer to the person you truly want to be. If the answer is no, then let it go. Focus on what truly matters to you.

— The only person you should compare yourself to is who you were yesterday —

Forget about others. Their lives, their successes, their failures... none of that matters to you. The only thing that should interest you is your own progress.

Look at who you were yesterday. What did you accomplish? What did you learn? What obstacles did you overcome? Now, look at who you are today. Are you better than you were yesterday? Have you evolved?

If the answer is yes, congratulate yourself. You are progressing towards a better version of yourself.

If the answer is no, don't get discouraged. You have a new day ahead of you. A new opportunity to get a little closer to the person you want to become.

When you compare yourself to yourself, you allow yourself to see the entire journey you've taken. You give yourself the chance to celebrate the small victories you've achieved along the way. Whether it's making it to the gym even when you didn't feel like it, choosing a salad over a burger for lunch, or simply taking a few minutes to meditate, every small action counts.

But when you compare yourself to others, you tend to forget how hard you've worked to get where you are today. You forget that every small step you've taken has brought you a little closer to your goal. Comparing yourself puts you in an endless race with no winner. There will always be someone richer, thinner, more beautiful, or more intelligent than you. And that shouldn't matter because you're only seeing part of the picture. You see their successes, but you don't see their struggles. You see their appearance, but you don't see their insecurities. Everyone has their own path to follow and their own battles to fight. So stop comparing yourself to others. Just set one goal: to be better than you were yesterday.

Be the "main character" of your life

Being the "main character" of your life is like being the protagonist of your own movie: everything revolves around you. It's your life, your stage, your glory.

In movies, the main character doesn't just sit around waiting for time to pass. They are determined, confident, charismatic, and they make bold choices to shape their destiny. They aren't afraid to take risks, but they do so strategically to move towards their goals. They have a clear vision of what they want to achieve and are willing to work hard because they know they are destined for success. This is exactly how you should lead your life.

But how do you become the main character in your life? It's simple—you need to romanticize your life.

Romanticizing your life means seeing each day as a new scene in the movie of your life. It's about transforming your everyday life into something spectacular and exciting, like in a film. It's about seeing the beauty in the small things. It's taking the time to appreciate sunsets, feeling the wind on your skin, savoring every bite of your favorite meal. It's believing in your dreams and giving yourself the means to achieve them.

To romanticize your life, you can:

- Start your day by listening to the birds singing
- Create a playlist that boosts your motivation
- Surround yourself with things that make you smile (set your favorite quote as your wallpaper, keep a vacation photo by your bed, etc.)
- Buy yourself flowers
- Read a book outside at sunset
- Organize solo dates
- Have your dinner by candlelight

The key is to make every ordinary day an extraordinary one.

— The 7 pillars to becoming a more charismatic woman —

Being a charismatic woman is much more than just about appearance. It's an energy that radiates from you, a magnetic aura that captivates those around you. When you walk into a room, heads turn not because you are the loudest or most extravagant, but because your energy, confidence, and assurance naturally draw others to you.

Here are the 7 essential pillars to become more charismatic:

Self-Confidence: Charisma starts with absolute self-confidence. Nothing captivates people more than a woman who knows her own worth.

Authenticity: Never try to be someone you are not. Be authentic in everything you do and don't hide behind a mask. Authenticity is what makes you unique and memorable.

Communication: Learn to express yourself clearly and convincingly. Your ability to communicate directly impacts your charisma and influence.

Empathy: Show empathy towards others. Listen actively and try to understand the people around you. This quality makes you more likable and attractive.

Body Language: Stand tall, make eye contact, and smile. It may seem simple, but it makes all the difference. People are drawn to those who exude positive energy.

Humility: Stay humble in all circumstances. Modesty makes you approachable and allows you to stay connected with those around you.

Determination: Persevere in the face of obstacles and failures. Your determination will propel you towards your goals and inspire others.

— Fake it till you make it —

Sometimes, to level up your life, you need to act as if you are already where you want to be. This is the essence of the mantra "Fake it till you make it"— pretend until it becomes reality.

Look at successful people. Most of them started by faking it. They acted like they knew exactly what they were doing, even though they were terrified of making mistakes. And guess what? They eventually mastered their field.

Start by believing in yourself. This is where everything begins. You need to have a deep conviction that you are capable of reaching your goals, even if it seems difficult right now.

Then, act as if you are already the woman you want to become.

If you want to be more confident, behave like a confident woman. Even if deep down you are terrified, take control and convince yourself that you have absolute self-confidence. Stand tall, speak with assurance, and step out of your comfort zone.

If you are shy but want to make more friends, behave like an extroverted person. Start conversations, attend group events, and show interest in others.

If you want to be promoted to a leadership position but feel somewhat underqualified, take on additional responsibilities as if you already have the position. Propose ideas, take initiatives, and demonstrate that this job is made for you.

This doesn't mean you are forcing yourself to be someone you are not. It simply means you are stepping into the role of the person you want to become. And gradually, it will become second nature to you.

Take care of yourself and your mental health

— Invest in your personal development —

Your personal development is your number one responsibility if you want to glow up. It allows you to know yourself better, evolve, develop the necessary skills to achieve your goals, and live a life aligned with your values.

To begin with, nourish your mind. Listen to podcasts and audiobooks that inspire, motivate, and educate you. Whether they are about entrepreneurship, productivity, self-confidence, or mental health, choose content that teaches you something new. You can even maximize your time by listening to them during your commute, while doing dishes, or at the gym.

Another tip is to use social media to your advantage. Follow accounts that motivate and inspire you to have a feed filled with enriching content. Motivation also comes from your environment, so make sure yours lifts you up.

Reading is another powerful tool in your quest for personal development. Choose books that push you out of your comfort zone, challenge your beliefs, and drive you forward. Three must-read books I absolutely recommend are "The Four Agreements," "Atomic Habits," and "The Subtle Art of Not Giving a F*ck."

Don't be afraid to invest in yourself and take courses to develop your skills. Whether it's a new language, a technical skill, or a passion you want to deepen, investing in your learning will make you more versatile.

And don't forget to broaden your general knowledge. Explore various topics, watch documentaries, and discover new cultures. You'll be surprised at how much it can enrich your conversations and worldview.

Self-confidence

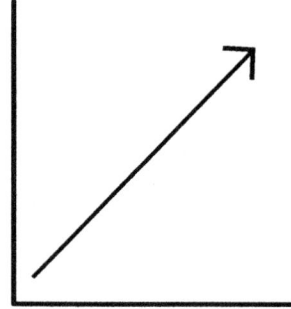 

doesn't mean you will never fail

but that you choose to become unstoppable

— Learn to appreciate the simple things in life —

Look around you; there are so many little things that can bring you joy if you take the time to notice them.

For example, consider your breakfast in the morning. Think about all the taste sensations it provides. It's a simple yet incredibly satisfying experience if you pay attention to it.

And what about nature? Take the time to step outside, breathe in the fresh air, and listen to the birds sing. It's amazing how simply being outdoors can improve your mood and perspective on life. It's like recharging your batteries by connecting to something bigger than yourself.

Then there are the moments spent with your loved ones. Sometimes we take them for granted, but they are so precious. Cherish the moments you share with your friends and family. These strong moments with the people we love give meaning to our existence. You see, happiness doesn't always lie in spectacular moments. It often hides in the simplest details, in the little everyday joys that we tend to overlook. Cultivating gratitude for the small things will make you happier and more fulfilled.

Make a habit of keeping a gratitude journal where you write down three simple things you are grateful for each day.

By focusing on what is positive in your life, you will attract more happiness and abundance.

So, what are you grateful for today?

— Find what makes you passionate in life —

When you discover what truly excites you in life, it gives you energy, motivation, and a reason to surpass yourself every day. You wake up happy at the thought of starting your day because you know you are going to do what you really love.

Now, how can you find your passions? Start by asking yourself the right questions. Try to answer these as honestly as possible:

If money were not an issue, how would you spend your days?

What makes you lose track of time when you are fully absorbed in something?

What topics interest you so much that you could talk about them for hours without getting bored?

What do you do naturally well, without even thinking about it?

What challenges or problems are you passionate about to the point that you are willing to invest time and energy to solve them?

When do you feel totally fulfilled and aligned with yourself?

What values are most important to you, and how can you integrate them into your daily activities?

What job would you do for free?

What dreams did you have when you were a child?

What activities do you enjoy doing when you feel overwhelmed by stress or pressure?

What compliments or positive feedback have you received about your actions or achievements?

What boosts your creativity?

It can be anything and everything: writing, dancing, cooking, teaching, coding, traveling, painting, helping, creating, entrepreneuring, or even a combination of several things.

Observe your interests closely. For example, if you like playing video games, what do you really enjoy about them? The competitive aspect? The sense of belonging when you play with others? There is always a reason behind your interests.

But don't pressure yourself, just because you haven't yet discovered your passion doesn't mean something is wrong with you. It can take time to find what truly drives you. The most important thing is to stay curious and open to new experiences.

Write down below all the things that make you passionate in life:

_____
_____
_____
_____
_____
_____
_____
_____
_____
_____
_____
_____
_____
_____

— Find your career path —

If you feel lost because you haven't yet found your dream job, Ikigai is your solution.

Ikigai is a Japanese concept that can be translated literally as "the reason for being" and it helps you find the career path that suits you.

The main idea of Ikigai is to find a perfect balance between four essential elements:

- **What you love**: These are your passions— what truly excites you and what makes you happy when you do it.

- **What you are good at**: These are your skills, your natural or acquired talents, and what you do well without much effort.

- **What the world needs**: These are the needs, problems, or gaps in the world that you are passionate about solving or contributing to.

- **What you can be paid for**: This is what allows you to earn a living, what people are willing to pay you to do.

Ikigai is found at the intersection of these four elements. It is where your passion, vocation, profession, and mission meet. Maybe you love writing, you are good at communicating, the world needs informative content, and the freelance writing market is thriving. Bingo, you have found your path.

Ikigai :

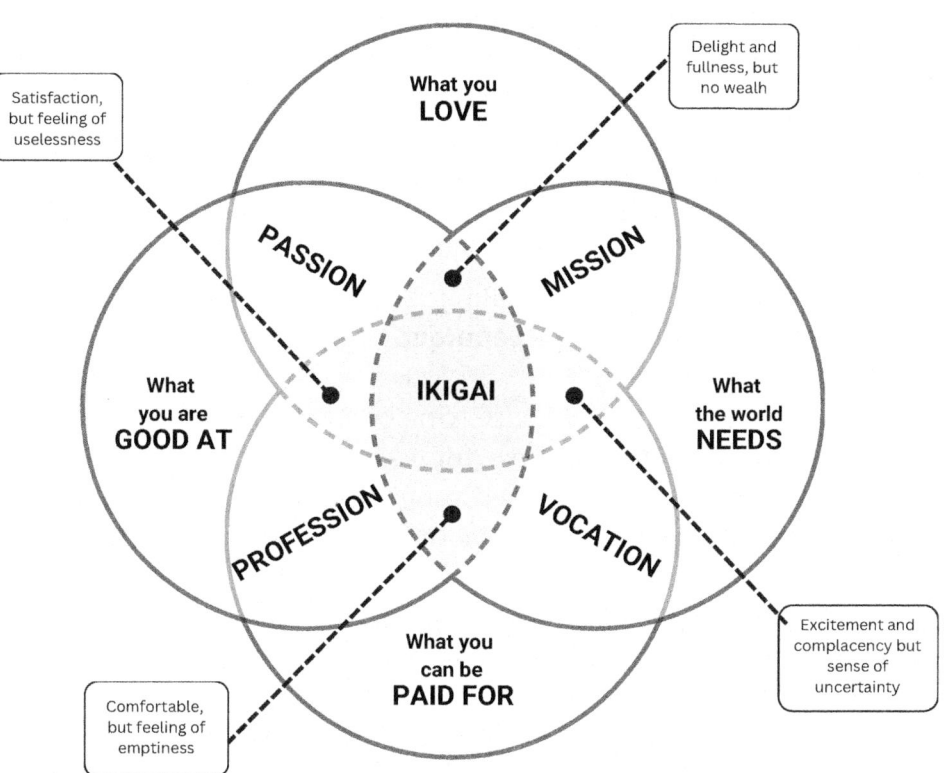

— The importance of sleep for your glow up —

We all tend to get used to that constant feeling of fatigue and take it for granted but it's not normal, and that's not how you're going to achieve your glow up.

You need quality sleep to function at your best. When you sleep, your body regenerates. Your cells renew, your muscles repair, and your brain recharges. By neglecting your sleep, you're depriving your body of this vital regeneration process. Your concentration decreases, your memory fails, you become easily irritable, and you struggle to complete even the simplest tasks. Lack of sleep also affects your appearance and even your weight, because when you sleep poorly, your body produces more cortisol, the stress hormone that can make you crave sugary and fatty foods.

Now, if you have trouble falling asleep, you'll love the **4-7-8 technique**.

Here's how it works: when you're lying comfortably in your bed, take a deep breath through your nose for 4 seconds. Hold your breath for 7 seconds. Then exhale slowly through your mouth for 8 seconds. Repeat this process several times until you fall asleep.

It's a simple but powerful technique that will slow your heart rate and calm your mind, leading you into a deep and restorative sleep.

And to really optimize your sleep, create a relaxing atmosphere in your bedroom. Use blackout curtains to block out external light, choose silk sheets, and keep the room cool and comfortable.

Additionally, try to go to bed and wake up at the same time every day to stabilize your biological clock. Your body will love this regularity, and you'll feel much more rested.

8 self-care habits to adopt before bed

1. Avoid coffee and energy drinks at least 6 hours before bed.

2. Write down everything that's on your mind in a journal to clear your head.

3. Make a list of your priorities and goals for the next day.

4. Disconnect from screens at least an hour before bed; blue light disrupts your sleep.

5. Turn off bright lights and use dim lighting to signal to your brain that it's time to unwind.

6. Reflect on 3 positive things that happened during the day.

7. Visualize yourself living the life of your dreams and feel the emotions it would bring you.

8. Create your own evening ritual to condition your mind to prepare for sleep (positive affirmations, meditation, stretching, etc.).

— Don't neglect your health —

Never underestimate the importance of taking care of your health. You need to ensure your body is functioning at its full potential to feel good about yourself. Here's how you can start taking care of yourself:

- **Get an annual medical check-up**. Schedule an appointment with your doctor each year for a complete health check-up. Monitoring your blood pressure, blood sugar, and other key indicators can detect health problems early.

- **Adopt a healthy diet**. You are what you eat, so choose nutritious and balanced foods. Avoid processed foods high in sugars and saturated fats.

- **Listen to your body**. If something feels off, don't ignore it. Pay attention to the signals your body is sending you and act accordingly. Ignored symptoms can lead to more serious health problems in the long run.

- **Visit your dentist regularly**. Make appointments with your dentist at least twice a year for check-ups and professional cleanings.

- **Exercise regularly**. Find a physical activity you enjoy and do it regularly. The important thing is to stay active to keep your body in shape.

- **Quit bad habits**. If you smoke, drink too much alcohol, or abuse harmful substances, it's time to stop. These habits harm your health in the long term and are not part of your ultimate version.

- **Prioritize your mental well-being**. Your mental health is just as important as your physical health. If you feel anxious, depressed, or stressed, don't hesitate to talk to a professional. There's no shame in asking for help.

CHAPTER 4

CREATING A HEALTHY AND POSITIVE ENVIRONMENT

Protect your personal space at all costs

Protecting your personal space means setting clear and firm boundaries around yourself, your thoughts, your emotions, your energy, and your time.

It means saying no when necessary, without guilt or hesitation. It's about maintaining control over your life and not being overwhelmed by others' expectations and demands. It also means being mindful of who you allow into your life. Not everyone needs to know all the details of your life or have access to your innermost thoughts.

Do you know how many people influence your life without you even realizing it? Friends, family members, colleagues, acquaintances—the list is long.

If you don't set boundaries around your personal space, you will allow all these people to enter and do as they please. You will end up doing things you don't want to do because you couldn't say no, feeling exhausted because you spent time with friends when you needed it for yourself, or being manipulated by toxic people.

When you protect your personal space, you show others that you are worthy of respect. You ask them to treat you with the consideration you deserve and refuse to accept anything less.

— Choose wisely what deserves your time and energy —

Your time and energy are among your most precious resources. You don't have a second to waste on things that don't serve you or that you don't want to do.

Think about everything around you. The people you spend time with, the activities you participate in, the projects you work on—everything. If something doesn't contribute to your well-being or personal growth, then it doesn't belong in your life.

Let's take a concrete example: social media. How much time do you spend each day aimlessly scrolling through Instagram or TikTok? How much energy do you spend comparing your life to others' or seeking validation through likes and comments? Imagine what you could accomplish if you dedicated even a fraction of that time and energy to pursuing your dreams or doing things that make you happy.

You need to learn to choose carefully what you will invest your time and energy in.

Ask yourself these questions every time you face a decision:

Is it really worth it?
Will it help me move towards the best version of myself?

If the answer is no, then you know what to do: move on.

Focus on what matters. Your time and energy are too precious to waste on things that don't matter.

— Stop saying "yes" when you want to say "no" —

When you say yes to everyone when deep down you want to say no, you put yourself last on your list of priorities; you sacrifice your well-being for the happiness of others. But you can't become the best version of yourself if you put others' needs before your own.

Let's take a concrete example. Your friend asks you to help her move on a Saturday afternoon when you need time for yourself. You're tired, you want to rest, but you agree anyway because you don't want to disappoint your friend. Deep down, you know you should say no to recharge your batteries. The end result is that you end up exhausted, frustrated, and regretting not listening to your own needs.

Stop thinking that saying no makes you selfish. It doesn't. Saying no means affirming your boundaries, your needs, and your self-respect. And you know what? The people who truly matter to you will understand. They will respect your decision and appreciate your honesty. Those who don't, well, maybe it's time to reconsider their place in your life.

Say no to things that don't serve you. Say no to people who drag you down. Say no to activities that drain your energy. You have control. You have power. And every time you say no to what doesn't suit you, you say yes to yourself. You affirm your value. You respect yourself.

I know saying no isn't easy, especially if you're not used to it. But the more you practice, the more it becomes a habit. So next time someone asks you for something and you want to say no, think about this book and say no. Don't make excuses, don't feel guilty. Just say no.

6 tips to help you say "no"

1. Know your priorities. Before saying yes to anything, always ask yourself if you are sacrificing your own needs. If you are, say no without hesitation.

2. Be clear and direct. When you say no, be direct and don't beat around the bush. No "maybe" or "I'll see." A simple "no, sorry, I can't" is enough.

3. Don't feel obliged to give a reason. You don't have to justify yourself every time you say no.

4. Anticipate difficult situations. If you know you'll face a situation where you'll have to say no, prepare in advance. Practice what you'll say and anticipate possible responses.

5. Practice the art of saying no. The more you practice, the easier it becomes. Start by saying no to small things to build your confidence.

6. Don't feel guilty. Saying no doesn't make you a bad person. You are the most important person in your life, and you need to do what's best for you.

— People don't need to know everything about you —

Throughout your life, you will meet many people. Some of them will even become your best friends. But you never really know their true intentions, even if you think you do.

You need to be careful about what you share with people because:

- The confidences you share can be used against you. Some people are not trustworthy and can easily turn your words against you when circumstances change.

- Most people don't really care about you. Many listen just to satisfy their momentary curiosity or for their own interests.

- The more you reveal, the more vulnerable you become. People who know too much about you have power over you; they know exactly how to hurt or manipulate you.

- People come and go in your life. Those you confide in today might not be there tomorrow, so what's the point of sharing personal details about your life?

Here are the things you should never reveal, even to your closest friends:

Your biggest dreams
Your greatest fears
Your weaknesses
Intimate details of your love life
Your family problems
Your personal finances
Your regrets and past mistakes

Keeping these aspects of your life private will protect you from many unpleasant surprises.

— Learn to enjoy your own company —

I don't know if you realize it, but the only person you will spend your entire life with is yourself.

If you constantly feel the need to be surrounded to feel good about yourself, then you condemn yourself to being dependent on others for your own happiness, which can prevent you from having a happy and fulfilling life.

Be happy when you're alone. Use this time to get to know yourself better. To understand what you like, what you dislike, what makes you unique. To reconnect with yourself. To take care of yourself. It should never be a chore to spend time alone with yourself.

There will be many moments in your life when you will have to be alone. You won't have a choice. And if you don't know how to be comfortable with yourself, those moments can become unbearable for you. Being comfortable with your own company allows you to become more independent and not need an army of people around you to feel complete.

So, what can you do to learn to love being alone?

You can start by regularly planning solo dates. It's like a date with your crush, but without him/her. Think about all the activities you'd like to do with him/her. Go to a movie, cook a nice meal, have a hot chocolate at your favorite café, go on a weekend trip, and do them alone. It's the perfect opportunity to treat yourself and strengthen your independence. When you learn to spend time and have fun alone, you become more confident and stronger. You realize you don't need someone else to be happy.

12 solo date ideas for quality time with yourself

1. A movie night at home
2. A picnic in the park
3. A shopping spree
4. A day at the spa
5. A gourmet dinner at home
6. A painting class
7. A DIY workshop
8. A photo session
9. A video game night
10. Karaoke at home
11. A chocolate or cheese tasting
12. A homemade beauty products night

Build a quality social circle

Whether you like it or not, the people around you have a huge impact on you. They can either inspire you and push you to become better, or they can drag you down and prevent you from becoming the person you want to be.

If you spend all your time with negative people, believe me, their negative energy will contaminate you. They will put you down, discourage you, and hold you back. But if you surround yourself with inspiring, ambitious, and positive people, they will push you to surpass yourself. They will support you, motivate you, and encourage you to pursue your wildest dreams.

Here's a concrete example: imagine you realize you tend to criticize and judge people very quickly, and you want to stop this bad habit. However, as soon as you're with your friends, they keep criticizing and judging everything and anything. Little by little, without even realizing it, you'll start doing the same thing again.

As Jim Rohn, a famous personal development coach, says, you are the average of the five people you spend the most time with. And it's so true.

I suggest you write below the names of the five people you spend the most time with.

1.
2.
3.
4.
5.

Do these people have a positive influence on your life?
Do they share your values and goals?
Do they support you in your projects?

Take a step back and analyze your answers.

— Surround yourself with people smarter than you —

Imagine you want to start in a new field, whether it's e-commerce, art, or anything else. If your friends know nothing about this field, how can they help you? How can they push you to excel, learn, and grow?

Now, imagine you hang out with people who are experts in the field you want to master. People who have already done what you want to do, who have knowledge and experiences to share, and who will inspire you to become better. By associating with these people, you'll start absorbing their energy, their skills, their way of thinking. You'll be constantly stimulated and pushed out of your comfort zone, and that's exactly what you need.

Maybe you're thinking, "What if I don't have these kinds of friends around me yet?" It's simple: go find them. Attend events, join online groups, take classes, do everything you can to connect with people who have succeeded where you want to succeed.

Of course, this doesn't mean you should abandon your current friends overnight. But be aware of the impact they have on you, whether it's positive or negative.

— Avoid people with negative energy —

You know, life is too short to waste time with people who:

- Constantly complain about everything
- Always see the negative side of things
- Tend to criticize and judge others constantly
- Are jealous of your happiness or success, or
- Belittle your achievements.

These people have no place in your life. And if you allow them to stay, their toxic influence will only intensify until it completely overwhelms you.

I understand that breaking away from these toxic people isn't always easy, especially when it comes to family members or close friends.

But you need to think about your well-being above all. Your priority is you. If someone is dragging you down, making you doubt yourself or keeping you in a negative mindset, then it's time to distance yourself.

— Don't be afraid to lose friends —

What you need to know is that the moment you decide to change your life, you risk losing friends.

Why? Because you're evolving. You're growing. You're transforming.

Some of them will be jealous of your ambition; others will feel threatened by your determination to become a better version of yourself. They'll remain stuck in their old habits, in their old mentality, and will be unable to keep up with your evolution. They'll be confronted with their own limits and insecurities, and will prefer to drag you down and discourage you rather than see you succeed.

But that's okay, because in any case, some people are simply not meant to stay in your life forever. People come and go in our lives; it's just the way it is. Most of the people you hang out with are there for a season, not for a lifetime.

Don't be afraid to leave behind those who don't support you, those who drag you down, those who hold you back. Instead, make room for those who rejoice in your successes, who encourage you to become better. They are the ones who deserve to be by your side.

Some separations

are blessings in disguise

Learn to stop giving a sh*t

— Never listen to criticism from people whose advice you wouldn't take —

Criticism—you'll hear it all your life. But you know, there are those who know what they're talking about and those who just talk. And most of the time, the criticism comes from people in the second category. Those who have nothing constructive to add to your life and feel better by putting you down.

These are the people who have never managed to realize their own dreams and envy you because you have the courage to realize yours. They always have an opinion on everything, but when you look closer, you wonder what they've really accomplished in their lives.

You don't automatically have to take into account the comments of people who care about you either. Why? Because not everyone is qualified to give you advice. For example, would you ask for financial management advice from someone who can't manage their own money? Of course not.

That doesn't mean you should reject all criticism you receive. There will be times when constructive feedback from those who know you well and have experience can help you improve. However, distinguish between constructive criticism and pointless judgments from those who are just jealous of you.

Every time someone throws a critique or a negative comment at you that affects you, ask yourself if you would take advice from this person, if they have the life you want to have, and if they are really qualified to judge your choices.

If the answer is no, then don't consider their opinion.

— Don't waste your time justifying your actions —

You may constantly feel the need to justify yourself to others, to explain every decision, every choice you make in your life. But you know, you don't have to. You have your own reason for doing things, and that's all that matters.

If you want to change careers, or travel alone, or say no to a request that makes you uncomfortable— do it. End of story. You don't have to justify yourself to your family, friends, or society in general. You have the right to choose what's right for you without having to convince those around you.

Your life belongs to you, and you have nothing to prove to anyone. Others can have their opinions, but it doesn't change your reality. You know what's best for you. You must do what you think is right without worrying about others' judgments.

So how can you stop this vicious cycle of justification?

It's simple: develop your self-confidence. The more you trust yourself, the less you'll feel the need to justify yourself to others. Work on your confidence by making decisions and sticking to them, even if it sometimes means going against others' opinions. Be proud of your choices, even if they don't please everyone.

— Better to be hated for who you are than to be loved for who you are not —

What's the point of hiding behind a mask all your life and playing a role that isn't yours?

Not only can people sense this lack of authenticity from miles away, but you also end up attracting the wrong people into your life. Those who don't really know you, who don't truly care about you. And even worse, you lose yourself in all this role-playing. You no longer know who you really are, what you really want.

Now, imagine being completely yourself, saying what you think, and doing what you want without overthinking it. Sure, some people won't like it. They'll criticize, judge, and even reject you. But it doesn't matter because while the wrong people leave your life, you attract the right ones. The ones who accept you for who you truly are, who love you for your real personality.

And even more importantly, you know yourself. You know who you are, what you want, and what truly makes you happy. And that's what matters the most.

Be mindful of the impact of social media

Social media can be a double-edged sword: on one hand, it can inspire and motivate you, introduce you to amazing people, and help you learn a lot. But on the other hand, it can make you lose sight of reality.

I don't know if you realize it, but most things you see on social media are fake. You often come across women with perfect bodies, the ideal husband, and a seemingly perfect life. But you must remember that behind these appearances are filters, staging, and photo editing. None of it is real. And when you compare yourself to these unrealistic images, you end up feeling bad about yourself.

Also, keep in mind that social media is designed to keep you hooked. How many times have you found yourself endlessly scrolling without even realizing it? You can lose a lot of time on these platforms if you're not careful and if you don't consume content wisely.

And then there's the dependency on likes and comments. Have you ever checked your phone every two minutes to see how many likes and comments your last photo received? Or deleted a photo because it didn't get enough likes? This is an extremely toxic habit that negatively impacts your self-esteem.

Social media in itself is neither good nor bad. It's how you choose to use it that determines its impact on your life. And we'll see together how you can use social media in a way that preserves your well-being.

— 4 rules for using social media positively —

1. No phone upon waking:

Avoid using your phone or going on social media for the first hour after waking up. At this time of day, your subconscious is particularly programmable. This means two things: 1) the content you consume has a direct impact on your mindset without you realizing it, and 2) it disrupts your dopamine levels for the rest of the day, pushing you to compulsively check your phone.

2. Curate your social media:

The goal is for your feed to contain only inspiring, motivating, or enriching content. To achieve this, you need to make a radical change to your social media. Review all the accounts you follow and unfollow those that have a negative impact on your self-esteem, that don't align with your values, or that don't contribute to your well-being. Seek out new sources of inspiration that share content that encourages, informs, or constructively entertains you.

3. Limit your social media time:

Monitor the time you spend on social media and set daily time limits. Generally, a maximum of 30 minutes to 1 hour per day is recommended. If you struggle with this, there are many apps that can help you reduce your time on social media and on your phone.

4. Regularly do dopamine detoxes:

A dopamine detox is a period of voluntary disconnection from social media to reduce the brain's excessive dopamine stimulation and dependence on instant gratifications like likes, comments, scrolling, etc. For example, you might decide to avoid social media once a week, a weekend a month, or every morning before lunch. It's up to you.

CHAPTER 5
DEVELOPING YOUR DISCIPLINE AND RESILIENCE

Create a morning routine that boosts your day

Your morning routine is when you take full control of your day. It allows you to take time for yourself and start your day consciously and intentionally.

A morning routine that works for X or Y may not be the routine you need. Ask yourself what makes you want to get out of bed each morning. If a good cup of tea makes you smile first thing, start with that. If you want to release tension before the day begins, do some stretches or a short yoga session. If you need it, take the time to savor your favorite breakfast even if it means getting up a bit earlier.

As long as it feels good and is beneficial for your mood, body, or well-being, include anything you want in your little ritual. What matters is that it puts you in a good mood for the day.

Personally, I recommend incorporating the habits from "*The Miracle Morning*" (a must-read book by Hal Elrod) into your morning routine:

- **Silence**: meditate, pray, or do some breathing exercises to calm your mind and reduce anxiety

- **Affirmations**: repeat or write your positive affirmations to focus your attention on positive thoughts

- **Visualization**: visualize the events of the day and imagine them as a success

- **Exercise**: stretch, walk, run, move... the key is to get blood and oxygen flowing to the brain

- **Reading**: read a few pages of a non-fiction book to gain new knowledge

- **Writing**: jot down your thoughts, what you're grateful for, what you're proud of, or what you commit to achieving during the day

This probably sounds incredibly long, but you can start with just 1 minute per activity, for a total of 6 minutes. The goal is not to have an extended morning routine that you can't stick to. If you start small, it will already make a difference. And if you want to increase the duration of your routine or add other habits that make you feel good, you're free to do so.

Now, it's time to set up your ideal morning routine. What habits do you want to include in your morning routine? What time do you want to wake up each day? How much time do you want to dedicate to each activity? Describe each step of your routine in detail.

My ideal morning routine:

_____
_____
_____
_____
_____
_____
_____
_____
_____
_____
_____
_____
_____
_____
_____
_____

Set goals and stick to them

Having goals is essential for moving forward in life. They give you a direction to follow and allow you to focus on what really matters to you. They push you to step out of your comfort zone and do things you might not have done otherwise.

That's why you need to set concrete and specific goals: **SMART goals.**

Your goals must be Specific, Measurable, Achievable, Realistic, and Time-bound:

- **Specific**: Don't be vague. Don't just say, "I want to feel more beautiful." Instead, say, "I want to lose 10 pounds" or "I want to improve my self-confidence."

- **Measurable**: You need to quantify your progress to know if you're getting closer to your goal. If you want to lose weight, set a precise number. If you want to save money, decide how much you want to save each month.

- **Achievable**: Be ambitious, but stay realistic. Setting impossible goals will only discourage you. If you've never worked out, planning to go to the gym 3 times a week from the start is a tough goal to achieve.

- **Realistic**: Know your limits. If you have a full-time job and many other responsibilities on the side, finding the time for an intensive 6-month course might be too much to ask. Be honest with yourself.

- **Time-bound**: Set a deadline. Otherwise, you risk procrastinating. Give yourself a realistic deadline and stick to it.

To make it more concrete, here are some examples of SMART goals:

- Save $2000 by the end of the year by setting aside $200 a month for a trip

- Run 5 miles in under 30 minutes in 2 months by training 3 times a week

- Lose 10 pounds in 3 months by adopting a balanced diet and exercising regularly, aiming for a weight loss of 1 pound per week

- Meditate for at least 10 minutes every day for a month to reduce your anxiety

- Cook at least 3 healthy meals at home each week for 2 months

Now, take a few minutes to imagine your ideal life in different areas: career, relationships, personal development, finances, leisure, health, etc. Once you have a clear idea of what you want in life, turn your desires into SMART goals and write them down below. From there, commit to taking daily steps to get closer to these goals.

My SMART goals:

_____
_____
_____
_____
_____
_____
_____
_____
_____
_____

— Keep your promises to yourself —

It's good to set goals, but you'll never achieve them if you don't keep the promises you make to yourself.

You need to be honest with yourself: how many times have you told yourself you'd get up early to work out, but when the alarm rang, you turned over in bed? Or promised to eat healthier, but at the slightest temptation, you caved in and ordered a pizza?

When you promise yourself something and don't follow through, you send two messages to your brain: "My words mean nothing" and "My goals aren't that important, I can postpone them." And it's a vicious cycle, because not only does it diminish your self-confidence, but your brain listens and records. It gets used to you giving up easily. And it becomes even harder to keep your promises and reach your goals later on.

Every promise you make to yourself, whether it's getting up on time, exercising, reading that passionate book, or working on your project, you must keep it. Because every time you keep a promise to yourself, you strengthen your willpower, discipline, and determination. You prove to yourself that you can take action, that you can trust yourself and your abilities.

This inner strength will greatly help you when things get tough, because there will be obstacles and moments when you want to give up. But if you've already proven to yourself that you can keep your promises, you'll say, "I did it before, I can do it again." That's resilience. That's the key to reaching your goals.

— Discipline > motivation —

You already know that motivation is crucial to achieving your goals. If you're not motivated, you'll never manage to change your life and habits. But what you might not realize is that motivation is temporary.

That's where discipline comes into play. Motivation is external; it depends on circumstances and your emotions. Discipline, however, comes from within. It's a habit you cultivate, a mindset you adopt, whether you feel motivated or not.

Motivation is what gets you up early and to the gym once or twice. But when you feel lazy and would much rather stay in bed watching a Netflix episode, it's discipline that gets you out of bed and into your workout clothes, not motivation. Discipline is what keeps you on track even when you feel like giving up.

It's like a muscle you can develop and strengthen with practice. The more you train yourself to be disciplined, the more it becomes second nature to you. You start acting out of habit without even thinking about it. You no longer have to ask yourself if you feel like doing it, you just do it because you know it's what you need to do. You create automatisms that keep you moving forward even during periods of doubt or laziness. That's where real change happens.

To become more disciplined, I recommend:

- Identifying your obstacles and blocks: what's preventing you from being more disciplined?

- Finding sources of inspiration, people who have the same goal as you or who have already achieved it

- Breaking down your goals into smaller tasks and measuring your progress to be aware of the path you've traveled

THOUGHT OF THE DAY

Your habits today define the person you will be tomorrow. If you maintain your current habits, where will your life lead in 5 years?

Stop procrastinating

Procrastination prevents you from realizing your full potential. It's when you think, "Why do it now when I can do it later?" but often, that "later" never comes or comes too late.

There are several types of procrastination, each with its own trigger:

First, there's **procrastination due to fear of failure**. Essentially, you delay a task because you're afraid of not succeeding or not being good enough. This can be linked to a lack of self-confidence or high anxiety.

Next, there's **procrastination due to lack of motivation**. You put something off simply because you don't feel like doing it. You know what you need to do, but you can't find the motivation to start.

There's also **procrastination due to perfectionism**. It's when you postpone a task because you're waiting for the perfect moment to do it. The problem is, often, the perfect moment doesn't exist.

Finally, there's **procrastination due to lack of planning**: you delay a task because you haven't taken the time to plan how to accomplish it. You feel overwhelmed and lost by the magnitude of the task, so you put it off.

Regardless of the type of procrastination you face, the consequence is the same: you push your responsibilities until you can no longer avoid them. And the worst part is that it creates a vicious cycle: the more you procrastinate, the more you develop the bad habit of not doing things in a timely manner.

On the next page, we'll look at effective techniques to overcome procrastination and regain control of your time and energy.

7 foolproof techniques to stop procrastinating

1. **The 2-minute rule**: If a task takes less than 2 minutes, do it immediately. No excuses. Reply to that message, fold that shirt, send that email. It's quick, it's simple, and it will prevent a pile-up of small tasks.

2. **The 5-second rule**: As soon as you feel the urge to put off a task, count to 5 and start it. No time to hesitate, no time to doubt. Just take action.

3. **Pomodoro technique**: Work intensely for 25 minutes, then take a 5-minute break. Repeat this cycle. It's scientifically proven: this method boosts your productivity and helps counter procrastination.

4. **The 5-minute method**: Tell yourself you're only going to dedicate 5 minutes to the task you need to do. Often, once you start, you'll find it's much easier than you thought and you won't want to stop.

5. **Time blocking**: Plan your day in blocks of time dedicated to specific tasks. No ambiguity, no "I'll do it later." You know what you have to do and when to do it.

6. **Ask a friend for help**: Have a friend set a deadline for you to complete a task. When you know someone is waiting for you, you feel much more motivated to act.

7. **Write a contract with yourself**: It might seem strange, but it works. Write down the commitment you make to yourself to complete a specific task. Sign it as if it were a serious agreement and keep the promise you made to yourself.

— The power of habit stacking to avoid procrastination —

Habit stacking is a simple but extremely effective way to help you avoid procrastination and accomplish your tasks. Essentially, you combine a new habit you want to form or tend to procrastinate with a habit you already do.

For example, let's say you hate doing the dishes but love listening to podcasts. Combine the two activities: play a podcast while you wash your dishes. Doing the dishes will become your favorite podcast session.

Now, imagine you want to stop postponing your workouts. Stack this habit onto an existing habit. For instance, decide that every time you come home from work, you immediately grab your workout gear and head to the gym. This way, when you get home from work, you automatically go to the gym.

And the beauty of habit stacking is that once you've triggered your automatic response, it's hard to break it. So even if you feel too tired to work out, you'll end up at the gym without realizing it. It will just become a natural part of your daily routine.

Once you've identified the existing habits you can use, simply link them intelligently to the ones you want to develop. In no time, you'll find yourself accomplishing many things you used to procrastinate.

The trick for it to really work is to choose actions that can be done simultaneously or naturally follow each other. This way, you're not forcing yourself to do something completely out of context. And for your new habits to last, you need to do them every day, without exception. The more you repeat, the more it becomes ingrained in your daily life. Before you know it, you'll be doing these things without even thinking.

Nothing extraordinary will happen in your comfort zone

If you want to reach your biggest goals in life, you will have no choice but to step out of your comfort zone.

When you push yourself out of your comfort zone, you challenge your limits. You force your brain and body to adapt, find solutions, and innovate. And that's when you realize you're much stronger than you thought. Every small step outside this familiar zone brings you closer to the ultimate version of yourself.

I know it's scary, and that's normal, but it's precisely this fear that tells you you're on the right path. If you're not scared, you're not taking enough risks, and if you're not taking enough risks, you're not realizing what you can achieve outside your comfort zone.

You need to learn to accept discomfort. To put yourself in situations where you don't necessarily feel at ease, where you don't know how it will turn out. That's how you learn to overcome your fears and trust yourself. Every time you succeed, every time you step out of that comfort zone, you learn something about yourself. You learn that you're braver than you thought, more resilient than you thought, and capable of doing things you never thought possible.

So stop making excuses to stay where you are. Because on the other side of this comfort zone, all the possibilities in the world are waiting for you.

4 effective tips to step out of your comfort zone

Here's how to start stepping out of your comfort zone gently right now:

1. **Identify your fears.** What exactly is holding you back? Take the time to note all your fears, big and small. It could be fear of failure, fear of judgment from others, or even fear of success. Once you know what's blocking you, you can start to overcome it.

2. **Start Small.** Every day, do one thing that makes you slightly uncomfortable. It can be as simple as smiling at a stranger, speaking in public, or learning a new skill. Every little step counts.

3. **Shake up your routine.** Shake things up by doing something different each day. Take a different route home, try a new restaurant, read a book on a subject you're passionate about but don't know much about. Always seek to do things you're not used to doing.

4. **Surround yourself with inspiring people.** As you know, your environment has a huge impact on how you think and act. Surround yourself with people who don't judge you when you try to step out of your comfort zone and who push you to try new things.

Stepping out of your comfort zone :

Your fear today   Your fear in a few weeks   Your fear in a few months

THOUGHT OF THE DAY

To live a life you've never lived, you'll have to do things you've never done. Be ready for that.

To succeed, you must fail

If you want to achieve your greatest goals in life, you will have to face the threat of failure and accept that it is an inevitable part of the journey to success. The most accomplished people, those who have achieved great things in their lives, all have one thing in common: they have confronted failure at some point. But what set them apart was their reaction. They took each failure as a lesson, an opportunity to learn and grow.

As an example, take J.K. Rowling, the author of Harry Potter. She faced 12 rejections before a publisher recognized her talent and potential. But she never gave up. She continued to believe in her story, refining her manuscript until her book was accepted by a publisher. And this is just one example among many.

Failure is your best teacher. Each mistake, each misstep, each fall provides a lesson you won't find anywhere else. Instead of getting discouraged, you need to understand what went wrong, why it went wrong, and how you can do better next time. This is how you hone your skills, strengthen your determination, and become more resilient.

Let me tell you something else: succeeding on the first try doesn't exist. That's why you shouldn't be afraid of failing. To reach your goals, there will always be ups and downs. Moments when you feel invincible and others when you wonder how you fell so low. And it's precisely in those moments that you must remember why you started. You must draw on your inner strength and keep moving forward despite the obstacles in your way.

Those who succeed are not those who never fail, but those who never give up. Never forget that.

THOUGHT OF THE DAY

The greatest successes are often preceded by the greatest failures. The more you fail, the more likely you are to succeed. And every time you fall, get up stronger. Because your failures today build your success for tomorrow.

Time
→

○ ○ ○ ○ ○ ○ ○ ○ ○ ●

○ Failure
● Success

Now, I suggest a little exercise: make a list of all your biggest failures, then note next to each one at least one lesson you learned from it. Every time you confront a failure, add it to the list. This list will allow you to see your failures as learning opportunities rather than challenges you couldn't overcome.

Example: "I failed my job interview" ⟶ "I improved my interview skills and now know my weaknesses to work on."

Failures ⟶ **Lessons**

_____ _____
_____ _____
_____ _____
_____ _____
_____ _____
_____ _____
_____ _____
_____ _____
_____ _____
_____ _____
_____ _____
_____ _____
_____ _____
_____ _____

— Celebrate each of your small victories —

We sometimes spend so much time dwelling on our failures that we almost forget the small victories of everyday life.

Yet, it is crucial that you take the time to recognize and celebrate each of these small victories. Why? Because it gives you the motivation needed to keep moving forward. When you realize that every little step you take matters, you feel even more determined to continue your efforts.

Each small victory boosts your confidence and self-esteem. You realize that you are capable of more than you thought. And you send a clear message to your brain: focus on successes, not obstacles or failures.

How to celebrate these small victories?

You can start by simply congratulating yourself. Take a moment to tell yourself how great you are, how well you've worked. You deserve it, so don't deny yourself this recognition.

You can also treat yourself to a little gift, something that makes you happy and reminds you of your success. It can be something as simple as a chocolate bar or something more meaningful like a piece of jewelry. The goal is just to mark the occasion.

Or you can simply take care of yourself and give yourself a well-deserved break to recharge and come back stronger.

Next time you achieve one of these small victories, don't let it go unnoticed. Stop for a moment, savor it, celebrate it. You deserve it.

After making the list of your failures, I now suggest you make a list of your recent small victories. For example, you might have solved a difficult problem at work, completed a workout even though you were tired, cooked a healthy meal for yourself, or maintained a positive habit for several days in a row. Every small victory counts, so don't underestimate anything.

_____
_____
_____
_____
_____
_____
_____
_____
_____
_____
_____
_____
_____
_____
_____
_____
_____
_____
_____
_____
_____
_____
_____

You've reached the end, be proud of yourself

You've made it to the last page of this book. You can be incredibly proud of yourself for getting this far. You decided to take control of your life to become a better version of yourself, and that proves you have everything it takes to succeed.

But this is just the beginning of your transformation. You've gained the knowledge needed to take your life to the next level, but now it's up to you to put everything you've learned into practice.

Don't hesitate to reread this book as many times as necessary. Go back to certain pages, highlight passages, delve deeper into the concepts that are most important to you. Each time you do, you will discover something new, something you might not have fully understood the first time.

Never forget that you are the only person responsible for your life and your happiness. You have the power to create the life you desire, no matter the challenges that arise. Don't let anyone tell you that you can't do it.

Keep investing in yourself. Whether by taking care of your body, nourishing your mind, or developing your skills, every little step you take brings you closer to your full potential.

You have everything it takes within you to become the person you want to be and achieve everything you set out to do. Believe in yourself and never stop fighting for what you deserve. The world is yours, and nothing can stop you.

I sincerely hope this book has taught you a lot and helped you grow as a woman.

If you enjoyed it, I would be thrilled if you could leave a short review on Amazon to support my work. It takes less than a minute, but it means a lot to me.

Just scan this QR code with your phone

If the QR code doesn't work, you can go to the book's Amazon page, scroll all the way down, and click the "Write a Review" button.

It's very important to me to know that the book has been helpful to you.

Feel free to reach out to me on TikTok (@glowupnewmindset) if you have any questions—I'd be happy to answer.